AF415795

As light into water

Piet Nieuwland

Copyright 2020 Piet Nieuwland

Acknowledgements

Some of these poems have appeared before in the following publications:

Catalyst; A Fine Line; NZ Poetry Shelf; Erothanatos; Indigomania; Sonic Boom; Fast Fibres Poetry; Brief; Otoliths; The Wild Word

Thanks to the Northland poetry community, ONEONESIX, Michelle Elvy, and especially Lisa.

Copyright© 2021 Piet Nieuwland
ISBN: 978-93-88319-50-8

First Edition: 2021
Rs. 200/-

Cyberwit.net
HIG 45 Kaushambi Kunj, Kalindipuram
Allahabad - 211011 (U.P.) India
http://www.cyberwit.net
Tel: +(91) 9415091004
E-mail: info@cyberwit.net

No part of this book may be reproduced or transmitted in any form or by any means, electronic, mechanical, photocopying, or otherwise, without the express written consent of Piet Nieuwland.

Printed at Thomson Press India Limited.

Contents

Aeolian alphabet

Today I do not know

How far the wind has come, or gone

Nor the weight of yellow tulips

Why herons landed in this field

How the leaning pines feel about solstice

Today I wonder about

Black hair in the breeze, the scent of her kiss

The luminous melancholy of luscious eyes

The sacred waltz of hurricane nebula

Vulnerable to ten thousand variables

What the wind looks for in the sky

When the sun picks up a zillion glassy flicks

As pale fogs flood through the world

Nestled in valley haze going green

Light in pursuit of her reflection

A sum of instants adding in flocks of bird

Wing flaps in their millions lifting

Daybreak music swift turbulences

On paths of least resistance

As light into water

The unrecognised potential of every hour is

parabolic moon flight over Tassilin'Ajjer / the seared sienna
edges

Sumatran jungles that melt billows into smoke plumes / earth
into air into earth

steroid fuelled furies of commodified experience / the fires of
perception

transcending the anthropocentric / the distance between us
and how close we are

escapes of elastic rock on fault lines / faster than sound speed

a dissolving view, dissolving view, dissolving

temple silence, in terraced pools, under cliffs,

tail fin flicker, yellow shining splash /

black wing, white wing flurry,

speckled, sparkle, and takapu flash / symbolic neutrinos,

 a night of pearls / spectral ice, luminescent needles

mirrored water, clouds of memory

in forest gardens of your desire / spiced bridal honey dew

white tulips, a dream of silver rice

possibly anything else under Corona Australis

Avenues

your mind wanders beyond logic

arcs of falling, over, in

the thickening world, its texture,

meaning of motion, its trace

not place, but zone and point

vectoral threads tied by magnets

electro parabolic hydrangea

dissolving in to violin concertos

on the dark morning pre-nuptial

woven breath shuttled

between mycorrhizal tissues

and the modest chemistries of need

in a democratic forest

taking the long view

where the future is a verb

In crystal fields

walking through fields of wild silver grasses

with Tzigane, gypsy of the transient universe

sparks shower from fires sharing the night

with darting glances time crosses the shoreline

on paths to the what is seen

binding edges of the what is possible

a horizontal intelligence of wings pass

through three states of matter, a camembert moon

describes its elliptic gradients of attraction

up into hidden thermal expansions of saline

waters that finger humid fertile valleys like Kiwiriki Bay

thick with nikau, pukatea, and puriri clines

crowded with epiphytic canopy gardens

impenetrable kiekie thickets

and agile red-eyed birds whose calls are

but memories of molecular alignments

in the resonant lignin's heartwood cell library

Manurewa

a drifting kite

on variegated particles of gravity twists

into a curriculum design process, its caresses

open memories, the tears

cushion cut green garnet drops

proliferate in subcutaneous territories

imaginary glass horizons and immense breathing forests

moments of Ceylonese blue sapphires invent themselves

in precipitous circumstances

over Rub'Al-Khali deserts

over phyto-planktonic curls and swirls

black marlins cross elevated thermoclines

coded translations of the atmospheric mosaic

playing at the elasticity of reason

with tredecillions of molecules

catherine wheels and spinning knot stars

ratios in a winged sonata

Points of no return

mist encircles the dispassionate hills

a yarn spreads to daybreak edge on water

the kissing minutes entangle

on the long body of the beach

with a melancholic moon currents rub through

before her he stands, word-less

inhabiting a shape at the point of departure

but with monsoons of theorems

on the quintic root of twinkles

de-facto acrobats in a syncretic shelter

the glance pianissimo at ocean lifting

wave fall in the heart of not silence

not quiet, the popular sky occupied

by pliable shimmer-shade shifts across

into a post carboniferous history when we say

what is and what it is not, what could be

and what is possible, what is possible here

on this shoreline what matters

for the children who are going

to the future of their children

and not coming back

tumbling down over the dunes we see

dance, frisking about in layers of warm

shallows shrieking

A distant certainty

not of polynyas, that will come

but of chandelle des six alight like pollen in a breeze

over aromatic mountain forests, fragrant archipelagos

her voice catches me, the scent

of lands inhabited by days, nocturnal horizons

hints of fresh flax, a vague familiarity

with bright eyes alert to signs of urgency

a wind shift, an orca fin

axes of pure whirling rhythm

as hours evaporate

in vivid ovens of hot bread

playing in the surf riffs, salty bloom on cheeks

like peach fur

Sarriettes

inhabited by silence and radiance we cannot see

all that has ever arrived here, become

the shape of leaves, pollen, exploding cones

gum resin-weep from bark, vegetal canopy

arcades, amongst darknesses

hidden from super-blue-blood moons, in curls

of algal arrays off shallow coasts

revolving through vast aquaria,

the distance moments take to disappear

in sounds we cannot hear,

groans that belie continental movements

wind in vacuous high places,

intimate close-up chats,

to the friction of bodies, ants gathering food

a hatching egg, the shuffle of sand, crystals, mineral flakes

the aromas we cannot smell,

pheromones of elegant ibis and cranes,

antelope herds and bees, what they eat

in places you've never heard of, the taste

of fruits in the Amazon, deserts on tundra

that touch

aquamarine nights of geometric calm

celestial currents in a river of beings

instructions of sunlight, their hazy echoes

imaginary fires of lush patience

The possibility of existence

Carry the sun inside

In the silver silence of an eye

On the empire of marginal unconscious

An intra-cultural soft shoe shuffle amongst hydrangeas

And glitzy market malls

A wave breaks

A spill of meteorites

when the depth of the shore water

Cuts the warp of light

is less than one-seventh of the distance

From space we can see

between adjacent wave crests

Sapphires and red sheds

The drag at the base of the water column

In the cone of ultrasound

slows this lower part,

On what were once navigable processions of whales

leaving the top of the wave speeding along

The spread of particles and ectoplasmic data

– but unsupported from below.

In the ecologies of language

So it breaks with the onrushing top curling over

A paradoxical melange

and beginning to fall down the waves leading face

Bikini brief semiotics, ikebana and sunscreen

which disintegrates into a white chaos, surf

On this, a notorious coast

Flotillas of spinnakers

Cumulus building on cumulus

To cumulonimbus mazurkas of lightning and thunder heads

Linguistic sutures saturated with brilliance

In the prayer of flesh the shades of her eyes speak

Everything with nothing to say

An incandescence of salt and silence

Beneath old growth podocarp forests

Next to the sea

Undercurrent

It's raining on basalt city, Auckland, Sydney, New York,
Mumbai, the grey circumferential continua disappear and at
Ahipara painted black are people at the edge of perception, like
moteatea for soldiers of Passchendaele, the language is never
innocent, we are poets and the poet's experience in the historic
continuum, the future keeps arriving, demands an urgent
subversion in the performance of leaf and wing that disappears
into the space before memory before silence knows it has flesh
blood and name when a beam passing through crystal lands on
a page, defines a defragmented identity an agitation of the
technocratic priesthood, a new condition of scientific
reductionists destabilising information marketers

Their ownership of discourse

The language never innocent

With cardamom and ginger

a malawah dish, finely spiced

on a Saint Cirrus evening

with Tuilerian flowers, a field

shivering umbels, black corsets and white knights

divine viridian sea shimmer's a laugh

sulky pouting flushed lips

on the infinite plateau of your back

starlight splashes

rose tears and ruby

the zone is summer twilight solstice

a dune path twisted with pingao, applauding

spinifex, we sink into nests of crazy kisses

creamy lace lattices azure fronts and soft advantages

seeing, in those ultraviolet hours

with feline eyes

yellow-grey fish singing ultramarine acapella

Digital sutra

A conflagration flares

on the whites of your eyes

in the circus of wind

circles of memory widen

to what we made of the morning

through frayed nets of curtains, unbuttoned

 all fall open to the hours

  caught, phrase by phrase

in each of the seasons, years vanished

 returned and again

  disappeared, track after track

skies exchanged clouds

fields left to flourish in wild rose brambles, day lilies

spring tulips and *Strelitzia* when the mythological moon

opens the starry canopy

and veils of heavenly rain

 echo with brass bells

  syncretic gamelan

In the atlas

Of vanished species, adze-bill, owlet-nightjar, raven

In the land of hearsay, speculation and innuendo

Deciphering ideograms in the silt and sand

With suggestions from Clizia of the piazza

Where, a cauldron of black pitch had spilled

From empires of the senseless and continues

To do so in the intermezzo

Between expectations and arrival

Where everything is alive and there is

No time to waste

Where your name is written

As an ancestor under a supernal heavy cloud

Next to a cottage

A trellis of bean vines and black berries

The violet itinerary of bacioni

At Sagaing

A pagoda on the Irrawaddy delta

listens to the blue pandemonium

The sweet orange tastes

              kisses of the sun

heart, jewel, bloom, star

Falcon curves soar

over mirrored black swans

the armada of clouds in the one sky

there is only one, the air, thinking it,

seeing it all, the blurring dark

greens, as time breaks over the

map of the world, clean bright moon

in the river, its semaphore articulate

on deeper water

this interglacial

fragile as dew

Extra seconds

From the lookout

bronze bells and jade chimes over twisted pines

bamboo groves, plum blossoms and ferns frond

       ninety million waves to the bay

a chittering of sparrows and yellowhammers

      songs to the eastern sea

a promise of magnolia blossoms

     the faintest fragrance

arrives over the horizon line, a widening grin

of mirrors blink, a distant lighthouse flash

    an empty silence

on the hidden parameters of a belief system

   statistics of blood and condition

dissolution of time in the law of catastrophes

in centrifuges over warm oceans

off Sierra Leone

In the clatter of family

In a crazed flash of lightning night pushes day off the horizon
edge, the northwest wind is pulled through trees, air breathing
in cycles of evaporation over deep forest canopies, over
oceanic multitudes, embryos of torrential precipitation in
monsoons, symphonic calamities, swollen tides, the simple
physical law

    Expands when heated, like metal

    Expands   when   heated,   expands

The chlorophyll sucks it in as a reaction, the photosynthesis in
your eyes deep in the pupil, a reliquary right in there with the
sound of wind through the leaves, the trees sway, the bustling
flax, the loams turning over, warmed, vigorous with potatoes,
spinach, prospects of tomatoes and zucchini, speculations of
magpie over fresh compost

    Asking is this the right way to live

The park

In the city centre

Is a pohutukawa tree older than people

Trunk wide as a family of four

> can reach around it, arms outstretched, as far as you

> can throw a ball, further even

It stands looking over the shallow bay

That was once below basalt

Cliffs, now a plaque park, memories to wars

Beside the tree stand others

Blossoming metro-red fuses when days drown

And people want to gather like gulls in formation

While the Hatea River wanders in to harbour channels

Unaware of questions its motion raises in modelling

Equations, how the flow breaks

Down, the mathematics reaches a point

Where speeds explode out of control, or infinitely tight

Whirlpools form and the silty mud

Its viscous mixing in fresh and tidal saline

Is impossibly difficult to account for

So we defer instead to accounts of Polygon Wood 1917

The rising notes of the trumpet

Ballooning their way in,

Into thermals rising

Over the cliff

Revealed by black birds and lifting wind

Girls with undressed hair

Changing with the moon

Eyes smooth as honey

Faces open with a surprise canna lily scarlet flare

A lightning frond on the darkness of a dress

Wet with a curve of rainbows and summer rain

Vanishing into the green / as your eyes have green

In our monotonous blood

That flows through our lips, our hips

Our thighs, limbs like willows bending and flexing

In tumults of buoyancy / racing towards a black lament

Of smouldering geraniums / of death flowering for love

In tents like exotic flags on riverbanks

That curve over and around life

A sky of angels illuminating

Evening spills a slow flight of herons into a cloud

Of silky mandarin cirrus / the heart still shouts the dream

Of electric lizards and frog bassoons

Stars splash in decillions of quavers

Brilliant with silence

The black shawl murmurs a rumour

You sit, pale violets at hand / not yet ready

Rotational hum

The earth's rotational hum

drum beats flashing ciphers on Tauroa Point

harmonic tidal breaths across labyrinths of sand

with your hair a gale windblown over violet azures

cliff track pohutukawa swollen with scarlet bee purr

the resonant echo of parakeet chuckle click, song and screech

hypnotic cicada stanza on orange blossoms

blackbirds staccato with starling fantasies

a yellow owl spins melodic elliptic variations on themes of ruru

the chorus line of surf sings hymns to the coast

a shrieking strike of a marlins leap and splash

when Concerto No. 2 hurls itself

in demi semi quaver furies on

to Tanutanu beach

Fragile mineral nights

Of moons collapsed by distance

And the solitude of an immense sky hanging

With a typhoon in hand

Its hyetograph on a heliotrope postcard

Her long black hair splits the afternoon in two

A long gaze drowning in the nuptial silence

Of a pair of eyes

We assemble impoverished shadows

Humid with the weight of tears

Drink in the view of subtle exclamations

Encouraged by laden plum trees and banana,

Glimpses of rivers that joins all the sinuous

Ridged horizons of prayers and flags

Of murmurs, rushes, zephyrs

Concatenations in the warming flesh of air

Its fine bone structure of fragments

That knit the winds

Blue serum

Gather on evening sea

A flotilla of lines wrinkle

night opens an anticyclone

window melts onto young foliage

radiant in soft dust

day unravels an unfolding

sheet it pours from what we call

curvature

of the earth, Hine-kapua reflected

distant between headlands and vestigial caldera

with wind from all compass points asking

what of the spherical hour, balance meteorological

that drifts across making notes

on its trajectory, in slipstreams of circulation

around isobars in cells, the pressure

between people, groups of people,

how close we can get here and still be ourselves,

and how far apart we can be

and still be together

Maternal substances

In foam that we abandon

on the edge, on the ocean's precipice

a morning of syllables

The tree in the field of dreams is occupied

its perfect architecture, leaves in spans of shade

a make decision web for a couple,

a family with children, young men and women crowding

to find a place amongst the twisted grey gnarls

that overflows with stories caught as fragmentary selves

Occupies fields of dreams in the tree

upon Te Turanga o Nga Manu Takutaimoana

what is hidden behind tattoos and bikini

inside bags and in the glances

mirrored looks behind sunglasses

their revealing anonymity

that hides another's sight

a stare

a hydrangea blue-pink calla yellow smile

of red orange bugle lily droplets

that spread across the families

bound in their play in sand at

water's edge riddles

a melange

of pa-cha-ma-ma paradoxes

In sight of hazes blown

Towards Mitimiti, the unknown coast, on that other side

funereal sculpture of orange sand wet with stars spilled

from rangi perfectly clear, crystals of pearly tidal

swirly whirls around the golden midnight

with the fact of a window frame in an old kauri cottage

overlooking a graveyard of hills, a mirror

water held like a flower twisting inside

strength fades, beauty too – a condition of echoless love

a trail in wind dissolved

in migratory fog descending the staircase

sacrament, turquoise rust spills onto white paper

an outline of bones mica-lea in your transparent cheeks

that hides a flood of filaments and branched nerves

radiant in the flesh of leaping droplets

striations in the cupola

our fingers bound in bacioni

at the centre-point of gravity

rivers fall from our mouths

Thunder clouds, Ao-Pakarea

In crumpled intervals of sun

whiffs of lightning report like dancing bells

in fractured cadences from the breath of black horses

on the fabric of water

amidst future words, hyperventilating

capacities of newness and holiday makers

at the beach, beyond cities

their exposed labyrinths and political algorithms

rising dust, rising again

in fragile breathing cells

enriched with the music of desire

enfolded in the gathering dusk

The wind-blown to tinsel

white explosions of green starfish

a gravity evading parachute of lines

striates the entire sky

guides pale drops to fall transparent

gazing into the space of memory

onto a rupture of moss, a nest of strings

trajectories of presence proxies and flax pollens

a comet burst onto the radiance of sun-showers

the verdurous expansion of korero entangled

on curtains of lush illuminations

fruits of rain

Behind pillars of black rock

In the intermediate world al-barzaq

I am the ocean and the ocean is me

a kiss dissolved into a surface, a waveform in apparition

folded into fractional space between 2D and 3D

a jewel in the circles of cielo amidst fires in the lightning

and its gleam

wherever beauty lies is a sign in the world of curls

slain by the sword of acceptance, the process of being

the life we are given at every moment

pearl shedding point cloud rain of tears

magic valleys of play in the secrets of time

slaves to intoxicating eyes, boundless illuminated treasures

that opens the fields of your heart

votaries of silken veils

billowing gold serums of quantum incoherence

the invented areas

Landing

After decades of postcards in the language of the wind

Earth is dark sweet moist and I am cloaked with hurricane

home is the colour of pomegranate, bursts of yellow peach

dense violet red tamarillos pitted black, soft ripe fig territories

tastes of thick black coffee in a late downpour

Egretta matuku descend from horizons of awkward lines

entering our heart's memory and fertility curves

with signals from future moons and the solitude of storm

surfaces on a wet night humid under sheets

where there is room for everybody

Together with your black lashes

The morning star and kotare sing at dawn

Beside the celestial pool, cypresses sway

The wave is a river in the sea of existence

A circumference of flowers that bloom for the fruit

On the bank, a thousand glimmers, a mirror

The heart is a current that flows haunted by lamentations

On paths across distorted areas of unnamed reefs

Hastening to a dialogue with the dead

With souls of the living, carnal and supernatural

The night beyond memory

In the soft instants when we learned

Secrets of evening wind, firmament of stars

Mythological decades

The sky explodes

Into natural sound-bytes, shattering pulses awaken, cumulus
into ultra-cumulo nimbus, hot, now cool, showerheads
blossom, bloom abundant, lightning tarantellas leap catapult
and leap in a surround sound boom box downpipe gush along
a plastic

       Pacific drum song

Splash, gurgle, rivulet be bop drip drop, alluvial masterpiece in
ying yang-ing, hydro logical cycles, the evaporation counter
point of rivers, of static discharges electric into cloud umbrellas

       A vortextural ambush

In the flat oceanic silence below Manaia

on Turanga o Nga Manu Takutaimoana

the warming land pulls a sea breeze in

clichéd glass smooth breakers emerge,

                picked off by a lone rider

while not busy, there is activity here, swimmers frolic,

horse riders gallop, karoro scavenge, oystercatchers forage

there are arrivals and departures, long shore drift

           and in the foam, exchanges of kisses

apocalyptic love is on tour and the elliptic moon on fire

La Nina leaves kororareka scores starved

this is not just a description of the world,

                some multiple realities manifest

or a context for the unexplainable, the hits and misses

what we get right and what is still to fathom

never-the-less this life is still unmistakably a biological process

with invisible vectors of wind and gaseous proportions

what makes up the remains of waves of quantum entanglement

here

Kia tupato

In the miracle of years that pass through the sand, the rough angled cliffs and skeletal trees, in the dive of kites and para-foil rolls, kapowairua cruise in the April of summer when horizons stretch to a thin blue sheet, when the sea at Pataua is pure clear fresh and hillside harakeke shimmers with the glow of warm offshore breezes, we bask in the simple physicality of sensations upon the skin, taste of salt, and the equinoctial afternoon is a frame sequence of children, their fathers and mer-maiden in all manner of poses and reclining not inhabited by algorithmic confusion nor vectorised bits of stock imagery as presence proxies but as humans silhouetted on the edge of a phylogenetically diverse functionally complex and trophically multileveled marine ecosystem where kaimoana gluttony is not tikanga in this sensitive cultural place, kia tupato

La Lauzeta

In this soft green world

more than the fresh opened flower she is fair

the lark, she spreads her wings for joy

sky falling

      falling sky

            sky falling

her whiteness more than ivory

ceremonial quilt and cloak

clear as an emerald field crisp of yellow and vermillion

with starlings on wing zippering across

her supple mane, mellifluous glance

as we read we become conscious of our own breathing

the last of what has passed and so with the present time

behind the silver-green of her eyes, tornadoes pulse

on infinite waves of rambling foam jumbles

post-cyclonic detritus of assumptions

the equinox conjures voices

from oceanic dustings of bone

we breathe in lunar mists

where all criteria of quantum linguistics

prove invalid

Watching the sky speak

determined not to leave,

watching the wind flower

on the delirious vines

watching the night sing

like a eucalyptus sway

straining in the velocity

the leaves quickening in the pixelated gush

present in this ordinary experience, anchored

by the ship bell's pure note

dawn opens its skin

Open to the world

a thousand layered eyes traverse the latitudes

and longitudes of memory acting

as if time did not exist, never

two glances meet without emptiness

burning ferocious enzymes and beautiful pairs

of impatient chromosomes circle in whirlpools

of magnetic fields an

intoxicating blush of faintly red

plum petals fill footprints

on the memorial shore a

calculation of the

gigantic wok full of stars the

sound of splashing water, the droplets flowers

of grief in

fleeting greens of boundless fig

leaves a tapestry woven

by the sky expanding its iterations

sharing the world

unable to be alone

On a weightless wing

we hunt the undertow

in the lyric of salt

in the memory of an afternoon

entombed by viscous warm

fluids, eyelids closing

over flagrant lustrous red

calla lily flames, candles

on the altar, she spinning

like a shining mirror along a

narrow path to the evening undress

of feeling, filmy fern

filigrees, soft translucencies

on the fulcrums

of equinoctial hours

A photosynthetic metaphor

The place, pixelated

    blood in the rain coiling

        through a gauze white curtain

shuttling in zephyrs, filtered by the afternoon

    a laugh breaking off from the language

        floats across the still pond, where willows

motionless over the black water busy with

    fritters of high cloud asks what is

        missing here on the bank, the muddled soil

piled with Poaceae

not visuals, but the philosophical process

    of optimal land uses

        a tracking shot framing it,

then what is out of frame?

    at a rippling of strings, congruence

    of exponential functions into a cluster space of limits

weight of her plaits and bubbles of song

what happens there in that river of eyes

a blossoming transparency, the eyes of ikawai

    the sky disappears

        with grey herons landing in the pines

gliding in, floating like sheets of tissue cloth

the garden of meaning

orchard of possibilities

the place of attention where sentences

find their place, hands open to a verb

    the black lament of a mother

    the black lament of a mother

A ying yang sacrifice

Something less is

the black veil, te aria pango

plumbing the aquifers of time

wind thick with the weight of air

the days fall like a hanging flag

to the nanny state for the rich called the free market

stars seed into the history of night

tanekaha drip with kokako laments

a black bull sacrificed to the earth

what we need

Te hana, the radiance

passing life on to others

in a forest of stars breathing

inventing days in bundles of reflections

the problem being your wealth, not my poverty

kisses like nets and the laugh of lunar eclipses

blushes of night wind changing the colours of leaves

sacrificing a white horse to the spirit of heaven

Amour mirror

Stellar scintillation riddles the sky

Iridescent butterfly wings gyroid in vermillion shades

Mirror trevally schools frantic in feldspar blue harbour shallows

A karoro murmation spills from the valley

Quark families dance in the ferny fractal fields

A neutrino flock passes through my left eye

Causes no noticeable discomfort

At a somewhere called Kekerengu P waves

Compress conglomerates in a shake rattle and roll

The olivine green goes on being through dissolving saffron yellow wavelengths

The ocean edge lacy, fragrant, swallows a screaming moon

A quardle aardle oodle aardle wardle dardle startles a magpie patrol

The day exhales

Hoya sweet nectar drips onto this page

Something extraordinary happened, in my universe, your universe

But not the universe

An indium morning

Between Te Whara and Paepae o Tū

Pohutukawa elbows knotted

With an asymptotic curve of fine holocene sands

Taonga islands drifting through a sifting, shifting lens

Where we landed,

Cloud caverns of frontal activity loom

A spring tide in spring pulls the dunes down

Ice plants melt in the white sun

In a season of fires

A red kete, red tee shirt

Ebony bikini, blushing cheeks

Red billed gull quartet

He korero[1], plays the ivory surf

The fertile ocean carved whakairo

Into literatures of foam and air

A pizzicato for children

Ngaruaroha, her cello, violins

Trembling like the toiling clouds

---

[1] He Korero Purakau mo Te Awanui o Te Motu: story of a New Zealand river. Steinway concert piano sculpture by Michael Parekowhai

Haeremaitekara

Kanukunuku

Kanekeneke

And yolo doves

Aroha mai, aroha atu — love received, love given

For millenia, humans altered the earth's surface

its hot clays furrowed in ceremonial signatures

these phenomena, a pyxis navigating to starry crosses

our souls at the zenith of superstrings

calm on the surface, beauty in slowness beneath

with toiling cloud bellies ripped

over deep sapphire

first petals, then cool rain

on the river flute

straddling the bells of time

the land a full breast dressed in shrouds

wings a-flight to memories gardens

in the piazza of our hearts

white swans at a black obelisk

and yellow doves

Around the candle

flocking moths shine

brown wings, silvery blades

angels with their proof of heaven

a full moon canopy unfurls

into the dervish dance of stars

as porotiti spin singing

in the emerald dawn

we make our words from bone

a language of birds

on the delectation of your vermillion lips

silken chords of sunlight pour

braided, woven, into the colours of clematis

falls tangled from a doorway

to the garden, plum blossom, lily, apple, a bamboo

point in the interval between the moments

we are overtaken

and nothing else matters

nothing

At the ultra

At the ultra-montaines crown in diamonds shine

where pale agile gusts speak silently with clouds

we sit beneath black blue green cypress sways

in supple flow with the lyrical universe

our talk, your mouth, my life's confession

not flame, nor carmine

of planting fifty fig and avocado trees

before proposing to a girl

faint as nocturnal mist

an umbilical chord

the yellow violin

stretched taught as a bow

plays

Curving lip that was

On the surface of planet earth

we walk wangling wiggled waggled

the moon is an island pancake

floating on infinite trombone slides

black saliva trails

pour from the luminous city

clouds entangled in aromatic silences

fall with dawn to the ocean

waves in a forest of leaves, weightless

raging verdelite greens / diners in kumquat groves

swallow saffron yellow peach velvet

on lyrical hips,

Anabelia flowers ferocious

a flagrant fragrant lily hot luscious

lip-sticked bone hard lusting

flaming scented

folded ripple waved

stop go street-light orange a gogogo

Gogogogogogo

In the interval

A meteor blossoms overhead

cartwheels a feather aviation star

Ngapukehau shrouds

expressions woven in the loom

of turbulent cloud web and warp

of wind threads twisted, bound

invisible yet present immediately

here, signatures of motion, toetoe

plumes write pages of clays,

in the silence opened morning tui,

evening ruru, the pace of rain,

its heavy imprints on Ngawha hot

pools, splash streaming their mineral

clay relax action, a sum of singular pieces

as pearls loosened from naked night

===

In this blueness over Rawene

we go there, when the wind drops,

poplar leaves on reclaimed edges,

ebb and flux of manawa, mangrove

===

At Waima River mouth

where Te Puhanga Tohora, Taheke Falls

meet waters from Puketi, Waipapa below

the ridge that shields, Papua New Hokianga

folds under gorse swarms and relic

radiata steeples hide pa and midden, rusted diggers,

worn out tractors, the midday grind

of beans pours out over the tide, align

of small launches, waka double-hulled

show the way, and fuelled

table talks drawl and gush

over art pieces in Auckland

babies smiles, nacho tastes

with chilli, punctured by the trumpet

blast of the ferry Kohu Ra Taurua

going back to Kohukohu side

===

In a reliving of puzzles

tangram shapes fall into place

like warm autumn clouds infusing the

aromatic air with blushes and stippled prisms

on a pre-Matariki weekend we walk

through streets trod by a great-great aunt, Ivy Grace

whose first husband Leighton Newlove, awarded

British and Victory medals died in Belgium

her second husband, Arthur Fraser

bought supplies at, now

No.1 Parnell, during the fall of the kauri boom,

when these windows watched rafts of golden

durable, carbon fibre head to global markets

and opening from eternity to privacy,

her green dress, unbuttoned,

for labour, the quickening heartbeats,

each moment caught, eternal

between the shining messenger of dawn

its return

Kahukura

Walking to the sea to breathe

    we go at dusk, dark

        waves coloured copper, emerald

take refuge in the night, your voice

between the mirror and the mirror

    stars taught me to write

a new semantic in photons playing on the warp

and abra cloud silk wind weft

    its dialect, weightless as

oceanic neutrinos and spring jasmines on

    a path to nowhere that overflows

with kisses and bejewelled aureoles

    laughing a luminescent charm

those kaleidoscope eyes, chocolate

    in a garden of pomegranate and orange

tulips and amaranth, blood

    in the clay of our flesh

Te Hau o te Whenua

It is Saturday in shed shade

a gyroscopic heat mirage pours over us with fizzing beer

the hills shimmer, uric golden green

in ridgeline waves and valleys

tidal cross currents and swells

early summer hay paddocks sweat out

from the piezo-metric surface

an invisible flow

In palaces of intimate dew

hungry pearls awaken to diamond thunder blooms

the ivory disc screams harmonics

Taking to high air

stratospheric Lixitae bubble with chordate data

cirrus red tongued horizon hangs by ghostly threads

viscous molasses black night

spills sugar star showers

Tauraroa walk

Misty-green islands / landscape of neurons

the day evaporates / summer drenched willows whisper

docile clouds descend

restless poplars clatter and clap / breathe in the wind

Wheeling gulls peel-open

a climate of new alphabets

ropes of wind braided, stretched

Eyes from the embers of years flower melancholy

fields weep, forests weep

the same green language on our lips

forests of curves meander

Walking, and the Tauraroa walks alongside me, walks

the Tauraroa, Kaipara, flagged by kahikatea

Al Khidr, the green one, my brother,

walks too

Scriptio continua

A sun of bees breaks open the day

a door of roses

light pressing on the trees

fresh bursts of sweet golden peach nectar drip,

the aroma, scriptio continua

the trees speaking with their cones and flowers,

seeds flowing falling

how the sky sings as the earth spins

branches conversing with the air

frictional dialogues

ripening rain

invocations of wind

fermentations of silence

the air as heavy as drowning

Under dacrydium

Sharp dark green spirals fall

Bark flakes to mounds

We are in the house

Hard rimu floors, the house

Of yellow brown red doors,

Heavy rough bearers and

Joists, the insides of finely joined cupboards

The cupressus that hums with Ruamoko

Sways with Tawhirimatea

Red pine of the high plateau

And steep wet gully, that echoes

With kokako and tui

Bathed in folded mists

Over tupuna maunga

Tupuna ngahere

Waking in the surf

Amphitheatres of wide eyed ruru

Surround our pillows

Gravid cloud cauldrons spill over

Masking Home Point headland

Te Whara and Peach Cove canopy details

Dis-appearing the ship re-appears

On a latitude of thought that reaches

To Curanipe, Chile

Another Pacific coast

It's too cold, too cold still

Yet maybe

Hesitate, hesitate

Dive into this surf line breaking in

A tumbling dump, no next one

Yes

It's a chill thrill to summers start

Again

Beneath the silence of light

And light of the wind

A wake of water in water under shadows of fog

An innocent path along the ultimate coast

Reordering language to trace cartographies of myth

With nothing between your hair and the rainstorms of May

Between night and distant sparks of fish

With a rose in the garden and a star on the door

Singing a song of song

On the parabola of instants

The first time ever I saw your face

Meeting Again

With our imaginary eyes

the balance of the world tilts

we take glances from each other

spilling into the spring wind

that opens windows to a lightness of being

and give glances to each other

with pieces of the past that inhabit

the what is happening

with eyes on the tips of our fingers

I feel you breathing

your shoulder sinks into the quiet foam

olive skin oblivious to the gentle flood of pathways

that pours from doorways

to the map of living

Without name or history

These are small things that surround me with happiness

the blessed endless black earth at my back and Sunday

with a blue sky tangling our veins

my eyes bathing in the sadness of wind

the pulse of ebony night that leaves my name

in the amniotic fluid of the evening sea

its tidal current of immense desire

your eyes moist with infinite patience

that leaves imprints

like small bony feet in the sand

In the memory of water

The day invented in the memory of water

A solitary yacht anchored in the bay

Loneliness on broken wings found in the west

The lecture notes on which his parents made love

Became the birth certificate of the boy

And in a more tenuous place, near the slope

Where the ashes of his father were strewn

Are the imaginary islands and hybrid architectures

Of languages that span pathways of migrating seabirds

And when the eastern ridgeline glows

Ectoplasms of the collective experience

Still demand their quota of faith

On this hill

To gaze at the splendor of a far-off star

A spectacle beyond the world of curtains

From the house of ample fluid space

Where right now the present

Past and future meet at the open door

And gentle offerings of night

Swallow greetings of previous inhabitants

When the world's population was 6 billion

Whose plastic spades became buried

In the sand pit, their playhouse became a hut

Where black hens lay amongst a scrabble set that's missing

Blocks spelling NGAPUHI or PAIN and HUG

Turning the pages of time tuituituia in histories of music

And the rain is no longer a-tranquility

But an unwitting flow of nights deep pulse

Dissolving the compass of glittering stars

That unveils down the valley of ferociously green

Savage trees that vanish into cloud billows

Like a broadcast of petticoats

Te Rerenga Kotuku

The archaeology of print photography of the red house and
blue and darkening curve of the sea, succumbs to the humidity,
its silver grains crumble, fine cracks form in the paper,

The desire of the eye to catch what it sees, pivoting at
memories border, the buds of scenography

The imaginary spirit, always at the same temperature as the
planet

In the fifth line of this poem was a peach tree in blossom

At the end young women swim in the surf

A gale from Antarctica has found a place here in spring, its
warmer

The static of breath imprints on the fabric of leaves

In the froth of dawn the scent of peach flowers explode

Syllables burn on the wick of buds, accents of rain and pollen
flurries

In this black language on the axis of stars lines in rebellion
breathe the atmosphere of culture

In the shallows, small things

When a blossoms fragrance falls like a meteor

A jungle tribe, whom I cannot speak for,

Bury their taboos and totems in river silt

From distant muddy fields

The lament of the mountains can be heard

Crying from the seven holes of bamboo flutes

With a clamor of drums and bells

Then we kneel to the south and pay homage

To absences of raised thighs, gentle epidermal curves

Of perfectly folded proteins, ambition, of egos dissolved into

The pleasure of auspicious clouds over a bay where

Salmonidae cultivated choose the scent of tides at dawn

The warm surfaces of summer oceans

Melodic beyond itchy heart beats

Wandering eyes

A cutting wind from all compass points

in mountains, at the catchment summit

in the wind, free here, at the start of time

below is the city market, mills of busy merchants

there is always a beautiful girl, French,

on the edge of a precipice, her lines float

in tribes of reflections, the present is motionless

in a pornography of pain and post-colonial resistance

the sultan forces the English imprisoned officers

to cut themselves with glass shards

…

pathways of paradox and circularity

in spumes and burial, versions of places,

stationary as a tree, mobile as a kite

of attention, part fibre, organic,

continuous unbroken carbohydrate chains

pulled by hunger, the insistent hunger

the fate of sunlight, to be that

Thanks to Octavio Paz

On the shape of waves

I listened for the secret of salt on both

Coasts tolling swells break peacefully

On these lonely shores plaited emerald

Waves the winds occupied

By pale lunar beings in net braids of stars

And satellites silken web lines of rain

Cello strings plucked cord of prayer beads

On spoked bicycle wheels the wanderer

Vanishes beyond the horizon accompanied

By a quartet of grey herons emergent

From twisted black trees wet with songs

That float on leaves washed bright

Riverstalk

In boundless silence

At the top of the world

Iridescent dusk masks catastrophic turbulence

The mirage of hesitant stars travel on their path

Living by an extreme effort of concentration

Over the silvery hypothesis of mesmerizing waters

On these mantled shimmering altars

Licking liquid forms of love

Meet me beyond freedom

Where radiance pushes through on superstrings

Of infinity, not pure, but changed

A silent dazzling flow of scripts

On the clearest moving waterways

Their cursive oscillations in varieties of variation

Tasselled fringes lyrical, inescapable

Te Tai Tokerau

We have come to the land

of the distant star

Where the moon shines

on a heron wing

Like rain falling on the women

        of distant fields

We have come to landscapes

        filled with tears

We have come planting orange trees

        lemons and naked limes

persimmons jewelled pomegranate and peach

Our path is a tapestry of words

We bind the hem of the kakahuwuru[2]

with pingao fingers

the poem weaves us

into the cloak

of a new horizon

---

[2] Natural wool construction

Our footsteps echo on the walls of a night

for songs, a night for songs

We know more,

    more than before

        than before than before

www.ingramcontent.com/pod-product-compliance
Lightning Source LLC
Chambersburg PA
CBHW060449160726
47992CB00003B/1151